CLASSICS

Great American

Short Stories I

❧

Willa
CATHER

Stories retold by Tony Napoli
Illustrated by James Balkovek

LAKE EDUCATION
Belmont, California

LAKE CLASSICS

Great American Short Stories I

Washington Irving, Nathaniel Hawthorne, Mark Twain, Bret Harte, Edgar Allan Poe, Kate Chopin, Willa Cather, Sarah Orne Jewett, Sherwood Anderson, Charles W. Chesnutt

Great American Short Stories II

Herman Melville, Stephen Crane, Ambrose Bierce, Jack London, Edith Wharton, Charlotte Perkins Gilman, Frank R. Stockton, Hamlin Garland, O. Henry, Richard Harding Davis

Great British and Irish Short Stories

Arthur Conan Doyle, Saki (H. H. Munro), Rudyard Kipling, Katherine Mansfield, Thomas Hardy, E. M. Forster, Robert Louis Stevenson, H. G. Wells, John Galsworthy, James Joyce

Great Short Stories from Around the World

Guy de Maupassant, Anton Chekhov, Leo Tolstoy, Selma Lagerlöf, Alphonse Daudet, Mori Ogwai, Leopoldo Alas, Rabindranath Tagore, Fyodor Dostoevsky, Honoré de Balzac

Cover and Text Designer: Diann Abbott

Library of Congress Catalog Number: 94-075018
ISBN 1-56103-008-2
Printed in the United States of America
1 9 8 7 6 5 4 3 2 1

CONTENTS

❦ Lake Classic Short Stories ❧

"The universe is made of stories, not atoms."
    —Muriel Rukeyser

"The story's about you."
    —Horace

Everyone loves a good story. It is hard to think of a friendlier introduction to classic literature. For one thing, short stories are *short*—quick to get into and easy to finish. Of all the literary forms, the short story is the least intimidating and the most approachable.

Great literature is an important part of our human heritage. In the belief that this heritage belongs to everyone, *Lake Classic Short Stories* are adapted for today's readers. Lengthy sentences and paragraphs are shortened. Archaic words are replaced. Modern punctuation and spellings are used. Many of the longer stories are abridged. In all the stories, painstaking care has been taken to preserve the author's unique voice.

Lake Classic Short Stories have something for everyone. The hundreds of stories in the collection cover a broad terrain of themes, story types, and styles. Literary merit was a deciding factor in story selection. But no story was included unless it was as enjoyable as it was instructive. And special priority was given to stories that shine light on the human condition.

Each book in the *Lake Classic Short Stories* is devoted to the work of a single author. Little-known stories of merit are included with famous old favorites. Taken as a whole, the collected authors and stories make up a rich and diverse sampler of the story-teller's art.

Lake Classic Short Stories guarantee a great reading experience. Readers who look for common interests, concerns, and experiences are sure to find them. Readers who bring their own gifts of perception and appreciation to the stories will be doubly rewarded.

❦ Willa Cather ❧
(1873–1947)

About the Author

When Willa Cather was nine years old, her family moved from Virginia to the Nebraska prairie. There she grew up among the European immigrants who helped to build that part of the country. In that sense, Willa Cather grew up along with the American frontier. She was the first modern novelist to use the West and the Southwest as her settings.

After graduating from the University of Nebraska in 1895, she moved to Pennsylvania. There she worked on a Pittsburgh newspaper and became a high-school English teacher. In 1900 she began publishing poems and short stories. Five years later, she moved to New York City, where she edited a magazine. She lived in New York for the rest of her life.

She is best remembered for three novels, *O Pioneers!*, *My Ántonia*, and *Death Comes for the Archbishop*. In *O Pioneers!*, Cather wrote about the pioneer families she had known as a child. In *My Ántonia*, she captured the life of the Czech immigrants who had plowed the farms of Nebraska in frontier days. Her masterpiece, *Death Comes for the Archbishop*, is about two French missionary priests in New Mexico. In all her writings, she showed a strong preference for the values and virtues of the past.

Cather believed that a writer's experiences before age 15 provided the most important material for his or her work. She is known for her strong characters. A great believer in independence, she once wrote: "No one can build his security upon the nobleness of another person." If you like to read about memorable characters, you'll enjoy Willa Cather.

Paul's Case

What happens when a sensitive young man is caught between two worlds? This famous story paints a powerful picture of the clash between dreams and reality.

THE MOCKING BOW ANGERED HIS TEACHERS EVEN MORE.

Paul's Case

It was Paul's afternoon to appear before the principal and teachers of the Pittsburgh High School. He had been suspended from school a week ago for his bad conduct. No one could explain it, not even his father. He told the principal he was just as confused by Paul's behavior as everyone else.

Paul entered the room smiling. His clothes were somewhat old and seemed a bit small for him. But he was trying hard to look good. He wore an opal pin in his tie and a red carnation in his suit jacket. But his appearance only angered the teachers even more. They felt it was not proper dress for someone who was supposed to be apologizing for bad behavior.

Paul was tall and thin for his age. He had high, cramped shoulders and a narrow chest. His eyes were his strongest feature. The pupils were very large and bright. When he spoke, he often used his eyes in a dramatic way that put people off.

When the principal asked why he was there, Paul said politely that he wanted to come back to school. This was a lie, but Paul was used to lying. It smoothed things out. Then his teachers were asked to state their charges against him. One or two matters of bad behavior were brought up. But none of his teachers found it possible to say their real reasons.

The real trouble was Paul's manner, or attitude. He hated his teachers, and he didn't try to hide it. All of his teachers were aware that he couldn't stand to look at them. In one class he always sat with his hand shading his eyes. In another he just looked out the window all the time. In a third he constantly talked, trying to make the other students laugh, while the teacher lectured.

This afternoon it was his teachers' turn to get back at him. They attacked him without mercy. Paul stood smiling through it all, his pale lips parted over white teeth. Older boys than Paul had broken down and cried under such an attack. But Paul's smile never left his face. Only his fingers, constantly toying with the button of his overcoat, betrayed his nerves.

Finally, Paul was told that he could go. He bowed gracefully and went out. The mocking bow only angered his teachers even more.

After Paul left, his teachers sat around talking about him. One teacher said aloud what many of them were thinking. He said there was something about the boy that none of them understood.

"I don't believe that smile of his is meant to be rude," the teacher said.

"There is something haunted about it. The boy is not strong, for one thing."

"I see in his records that he was born in Colorado," another teacher said. "Just a few months later, his mother died. I don't know what to make of it. But there is something *wrong* about the fellow."

His teachers were not happy when they left the building. They felt ashamed to have attacked Paul the way they had. After all, he was still only a boy. Perhaps they had been too harsh. It was as if a miserable street cat had been jumped by a band of lions.

As for Paul, he ran down the hall whistling to himself. He wished that his teachers were there to see how light-hearted he was. By now it was late afternoon. Paul was on duty that evening as an usher at Carnegie Hall. So he decided he would not go home to supper.

When he reached the music hall, the doors were still closed. Paul decided to go up to the picture gallery. The place was always empty at this hour. Paul

loved to look at the paintings there. His
favorites were the Paris street scenes
and the waters of Venice. No one was
there but one old guard. He sat in a
corner with a black patch over one eye
and the other eye closed. Paul sat down
and lost himself in one special painting.
When he looked at his watch again, it
was after 7:00 P.M. He jumped up and
ran downstairs to the ushers' dressing
room.

When he arrived, several of the boys
were already there. Paul quickly put on
his uniform. It fit well, and Paul liked
the way he looked in it. He always got
excited when he dressed. The sounds of
the musicians warming up in the next
room added to his pleasure. Tonight he
was even more excited than usual.

Paul hurried out to the front of the
house to seat the early comers. He was a
very good usher. He was polite, and he
always smiled as he showed people to
their seats. All the people in his section
thought he was a charming boy.

As the house filled, Paul grew more excited. It was as if this were a great party and he were the host.

Soon the music began. Paul sank into one of the rear seats with a sigh of relief. He quickly lost himself—just as he had done earlier in the picture gallery. It wasn't so much that he liked the kind of music being played. But the first sound of the instruments always seemed to free him somehow. At those moments, he felt a sudden love for life. He was in a different world.

When the concert ended, Paul walked outside. He stood in front of the hall and stared across at the Schenley Hotel. The building stood out big and square through the fine rain that had started to fall. The windows of its 12 floors seemed to glow like those of a lighted cardboard house under a Christmas tree. Paul knew that all the best actors and singers stayed there when they were in town. The boy had often hung about the hotel, watching the people go in and out. How he longed to go in! Then he could leave his schoolmasters and all his worries behind him forever.

Suddenly it began to rain harder. Paul's boots began to let in water. His light coat was clinging wet about him. The concert hall was now dark. He wondered if he would always be on the outside, looking in at the light. Slowly, Paul turned and walked toward the streetcar tracks. The end had to come sometime.

Half an hour later Paul reached his neighborhood. He got off the streetcar and went slowly down one of the side streets. It was a street where all the houses were exactly alike. Middle-class businessmen raised large families of children here. All the children went to Sunday school and were interested in arithmetic. And all of them were as exactly alike as their homes.

Paul walked up his street, Cordelia Street, with the same feeling he always had—disgust. His home was next door to the minister's. As he came up to it, he felt himself sinking back into ugliness.

The closer he got to the house, the more he felt he couldn't face it. There was the ugly room he slept in. There was the cold bathroom with the dirty tub, cracked mirror, and dripping faucets. Most of all, there was his father. The man would be waiting at the top of the stairs with a lot of questions and that angry look on his face. Paul felt the waters closing over his head.

The boy stopped in front of the door. He knew he couldn't face his father tonight. He could not sleep on that awful bed. He would not go in. He'd tell his father that he had no car fare. He'd say it had been raining too hard to walk home. He'd say that he had stayed the night with one of the other ushers.

But Paul was wet and cold. He went around to the back of the house. There he tried one of the basement windows and found it open. He raised it quietly and scrambled down the wall to the floor. Then he held his breath and listened. The floor above him was silent, and there was no sound on the stairs. Paul found a wooden box and carried it over to the furnace. There he sat down, and in a few moments he was sound asleep.

The following Sunday was a beautiful day. The chilly November weather was broken by a last flash of Indian summer. In the morning Paul had to go to church and Sunday school, as always. On nice Sunday afternoons like this one, the people of Cordelia Street were always outdoors. The grown-ups sat on their front "stoops" and talked to their neighbors on the next stoop. The children played in the streets. There were so many of them that the place looked like a kindergarten playground.

All afternoon Paul sat on the lowest step of his stoop, staring into the street. His father sat on the top step. He was talking to a young man who was playing with a baby on his knee. This young man was often held up to Paul as a role model. It was Paul's father's dearest hope that Paul could turn out like him. The young man was a clerk to the president of a great steel corporation. He was only 26, but he had already settled down. He was married and had four children. He was looked upon as a "young man with a future."

After supper that evening Paul helped dry the dishes. Then he asked his father whether he could visit a schoolmate to get some help in geometry. That meant he had to ask for car fare, too. His father never liked to hear requests for money, no matter how little. But he gave him the dime. He wasn't a poor man, but he still wanted to come up in the world. He only let Paul work as an usher because he thought the boy should be earning a little.

Paul ran upstairs to clean up. Then he left the house with his geometry book under his arm. The moment he got off Cordelia Street, he got on a street-car headed for downtown. He began to live again.

Paul knew the leading young actor who performed at one of the big downtown theaters. He had told Paul to drop in at Sunday night rehearsals anytime. For more than a year, Paul had spent every moment he could hanging around Charley Edwards's dressing room.

It was at the theater and at Carnegie Hall that Paul really lived. This was his own fairy tale. It was like a secret love. The moment he came into the stage area, he felt like a prisoner set free. Somehow it seemed that even he might say or do wonderful, poetic things in that magic place. In the outside world, everything natural seemed hard and mean and ugly. Only in the make-believe world of the theater could he see beauty.

Many of Paul's teachers thought that his mind had been affected by reading wild stories. But the truth was that he hardly ever read at all. The books at home held no interest for him. And neither did the ones his friends urged him to read. He got what he wanted much more quickly from music—any kind of music at all. It was the spark of his imagination. Just one sound could cause him to make plots and pictures of his own.

It was also true that he was not stage struck. He had no wish to be an actor, any more than he wanted to be a musician. He had no need to *do* any of these things. What he wanted was to see, to be in the atmosphere of it all. He wanted to float on the wave of it, to be carried away from everything else.

Things got worse with Paul at school. Somehow he felt a great need to show his teachers how much he disliked them and their lectures. And he also had to let them know how much he was appreciated elsewhere. He said he had no time to fool with geometry. He said that he was helping the people down at the theater—they were old friends of his.

Finally the principal went to Paul's father. Paul was taken out of school and put to work. The manager at Carnegie Hall was told to get another usher. The doorkeeper at the theater was told not to let him in anymore. And Charley Edwards sadly promised Paul's father that he would not see the boy again. Everyone agreed that Paul's was a bad case.

The eastbound train traveled through a blinding January snowstorm. A gray dawn was beginning to break when the engine whistled just outside of Newark. Paul awoke with a start. He'd had a restless sleep, sitting up in his seat. Now he rubbed the fogged-over window glass and looked out. The snow drifts already lay deep in the fields and along the fences.

When he arrived at Jersey City, Paul hurried through his breakfast. He was nervous and kept a sharp eye about him. After he left the train station, he took a cab to a men's clothing store. There he spent two hours choosing a new suit. Then he went on to a hat store, a shoe store, and a jeweler's.

It was early afternoon when he arrived at New York's famous Waldorf Hotel. At the front desk, he told the clerk that he was from Washington. He said that his parents had been traveling in Europe and that he had come to greet them on their return. No one doubted his story. It helped that he offered to pay in advance for his room.

Not once, but a hundred times, Paul had planned this entry into New York. He had gone over every detail of it with Charley Edwards. At home, he had a scrapbook full of pages with descriptions of New York hotels. So the Waldorf held no surprises for him. When he was shown to his room, everything was just as he had pictured it.

Paul ordered flowers for the room and then tumbled into a hot bath. When he came out of the bathroom in his new silk underwear, he looked out the window. The snow was whirling so wildly that he could barely see across the street. Inside, the air was soft and fresh. He sat down on the couch and thought about the last 24 hours.

It had been so simple, really. They had shut him out of the theater and concert hall. And once they had taken away his only joy, they had really made his decision for him. The rest was just a matter of opportunity.

The one thing that surprised him was his own courage. He knew very well that he had always been trapped by fear. Until now, he could not remember a time when he was not deeply afraid of something. Even when he was a little boy, it was always there—behind him, or in front, or on either side. There had always been that "shadow" in the corner, the dark place where he dare not look. And there had been the feeling that something was watching him. Now, for the first time, he felt as if he had conquered that "thing" in the corner.

Yet it had only been a day since his world had changed. Yesterday afternoon he had been sent to the bank with

Denny & Carson's deposit, as usual. But this time he had been told to leave the company's book to be balanced. There was more than $2,000 in checks, and another $1,000 in cash. How easy it had been! He had simply taken the cash from the book and put it in his pocket. Then he had made out a new deposit slip for just the $2,000.

Back at the office he had finished his work without looking nervous. Then he had asked for a full day off the next day, Saturday. He knew the bank book would not be returned to the company until Monday or Tuesday. And his father would be out of town all next week. That evening he boarded the night train for New York.

How very easy it had been! Here he was, the thing done. It was not a dream, and there would be no awakening. There would be no figure at the top of the stairs. He watched the snow flakes whirling by his window until he fell asleep.

When he woke up, it was 3:00 in the afternoon. He jumped up. Half of one of his precious days was already gone! He spent more than an hour dressing. Then he checked himself carefully in the mirror. Everything was quite perfect. He was exactly the kind of boy he wanted to be.

Paul went downstairs and took a cab up Fifth Avenue toward Central Park. He saw that the snow had let up. Boys in heavy coats were shoveling off the doorsteps. On many corners, there were stands with whole flower gardens blooming under glass cases. The snow flakes had stuck to the sides of the cases, making the flowers look even more beautiful. Central Park itself was a winter wonderland.

A few hours later, Paul returned to the hotel to have dinner. He could hear music floating up to him through the elevator shaft. His head began to spin as he walked through the hallway. The bright lights, the people talking, the smell of perfumes—they were almost too much for him. He wondered if he could stand it. But the feeling lasted only for a moment. *These were his own people,* he told himself. He walked slowly around the hotel, through the writing rooms, smoking rooms, and reception rooms. He felt as if he were exploring a palace, built just for him.

In the dining room, Paul sat down at a table near a window. He looked around at the flowers, the white tablecloths, and the many colored glasses. Again he heard the sounds of the orchestra. All of his senses were flooded. This was what the whole world was fighting for, he thought. This was what the struggle was all about.

He doubted the reality of his past life. Had he ever known a place called Cordelia Street? He could hardly remember that place where all the tired-looking businessmen had the smell of cooking in their clothes. That belonged to another time and country. Hadn't he always been here, night after night, from as far back as he could remember? Somehow he was sure that he had.

Paul was not the least bit lonely. He had no special wish to meet or know any of these people. All he wanted was the right to be there—to look on and to think about everything around him. No longer did he have a strong need to prove himself. He felt that his surroundings explained him. Here, nobody questioned his dress or his manner. He looked down at his clothes. He knew it would be impossible for anyone to embarrass him.

By Sunday morning the city was almost snow-bound. Paul had a late breakfast. In the afternoon he met a wild boy from San Francisco. The boy was a freshman at Yale who had come to town for some fun over the weekend. After dinner the two boys went out to see the night side of the town. They didn't return to the hotel until 7:00 the next morning. Paul went right to bed and didn't wake up until 2:00 in the afternoon. When he did, he was very thirsty and dizzy. He ordered some ice water, coffee, and the Pittsburgh newspapers.

No one who worked for the hotel ever suspected a thing. Paul behaved well and in no way called attention to himself. His greatest joy was to watch the gray winter twilights from his sitting room. He loved smelling the fresh flowers there, and most of all, he loved his sense of power.

He could never remember a time when he had felt so at peace with himself. There was no need to lie anymore. He had never enjoyed lying, even at school. The only reason he had lied was to be noticed and admired. And to prove that he was different from other Cordelia Street boys.

Now that he was away from all that, he felt a good deal more like a man. Now he could, as his actor friends would say, "dress the part." In no way did he feel sorry for stealing the money. His golden days went by without a shadow. And he made each one as perfect as he could.

On his eighth day in New York, a story about him was written up in the Pittsburgh newspapers. His company, Denny & Carson, stated that Paul's father had repaid the stolen money. The company had no plans to bring charges against the boy. The minister who lived next door had been interviewed, too. He said that he still had high hopes of bringing the motherless boy back to the good life. Paul's Sunday school teacher said she would try her best to see to it. A rumor had reached Pittsburgh that Paul had been seen in a New York hotel. The story said that Paul's father had gone East to find him and bring him back home.

When he read the news, Paul sank onto a chair, weak to the knees. It was to be worse than jail, even. The drowning waters of Cordelia Street would close over him finally and forever. His old life came rushing back to him. The boredom, the peeling wallpaper, the endless gray days stretched out before him. He had the old feeling that the music had stopped playing, that the play was over. He broke out in a sweat, jumped up, and looked in a mirror. Then he winked at himself. Suddenly his mood changed as he recalled his old belief in miracles. Then he quickly dressed and ran whistling down the hallway to the elevator.

When Paul entered the dining room, the music swelled up to greet him. He sat down and began to think. For the first time, he realized he could have done the whole thing more wisely. He might have caught a ship for Europe or South America and gotten clean away. But the other side of the world had seemed too far away. He could not have waited for it. His need had been too great. No, he would do it all again the same way. He looked around the beautiful dining room. Yes, it had all been worth it.

The next morning Paul woke up with a painful throbbing in his head and feet. He had thrown himself across the bed without undressing and slept with his shoes on. His arms and legs felt very heavy. His tongue and throat were dry. Then, suddenly, his head began to clear. He lay still and let his thoughts wash over him.

His father was already in New York, Paul told himself. What could he do? He had less than $100 left. Now he knew, more than ever, that money was everything. It was the wall that stood between everything he hated and everything he wanted.

The adventure was winding itself up. He knew that it would—even from his first wonderful day in New York. He had even thought of a way to snap the thread. It lay on his dressing table now. Last night he had taken the gun out to study it. But the shiny metal hurt his eyes and he didn't like the looks of it or the feel of it in his hand.

Paul got up and moved about painfully. He felt sick to his stomach, yet somehow he was calm. And he was not afraid of anything. Perhaps it was because he had looked into the dark corner at last. What he saw there was bad enough—but not as bad as his long fear of it had been. Now everything was clear to him. He felt that at last he had lived the sort of life he was meant to live. For half an hour he sat staring at the gun. But he told himself that was not the way. So he went downstairs and left the hotel.

Paul got off the train at Newark, and then he took a cab out of town. He told the driver to follow the Pennsylvania railroad tracks. The snow lay heavy on the roads and had drifted deep in the open field. When they were well into the country, Paul let the cab go. Then he walked along the tracks, his mind wandering.

He saw that the flower in his buttonhole was drooping from the cold. Its red glory was all over. He remembered the flower stands he had seen on his first night in New York. All those flowers must be gone now, too. It was a losing game in the end, he thought. Beauty has to give in to the rules by which the world is run. He took the flower from his coat and carefully covered it up with snow.

At last Paul reached a little hillside where the tracks ran about 20 feet below. He stopped and sat down. He was so tired, he soon fell asleep.

The sound of a coming train woke him. Paul jumped to his feet. He was afraid he would be too late to carry out his plan. For a moment he stood watching the oncoming engine. His lips were drawn away from his chattering teeth in a frightened smile. He looked around as though he were being watched. Then, when the right moment came, he jumped.

As he fell, the foolishness of what he had done became clear to him. The pictures of his imagined future flashed through his brain. He saw the blue ocean water, the yellow desert sands—all that was left unseen and undone.

Paul felt something strike his chest. He felt his body being thrown swiftly through the air, far and fast. Then, as his body fell back towards earth, everything went totally black, and Paul dropped back into the immense design of things.

The Sculptor's Funeral

How does a small town pay tribute to its most famous son? Or will jealousy and narrow-mindedness forbid any tribute at all?

THE COFFIN WAS TAKEN DOWN FROM THE TRAIN AND
PLACED ON THE SNOWY PLATFORM.

The Sculptor's Funeral

A group of men stood by the train station of a little Kansas town. They were waiting for the night train, which was already 20 minutes late. The snow had fallen thick over everything and the night air was very cold. Trying to keep warm, the men on the platform stood first on one foot and then on the other.

They spoke to each other in low tones, moving about restlessly. No one seemed to know what was expected. Just one man seemed to know exactly why he was there. He kept apart from the rest. Again and again, he walked to the far end of the platform and then returned to the station door. As he walked, his thick shoulders hunched forward and his chin was sunk in his overcoat collar. Soon he was approached by a tall, thin old man dressed in a faded Grand Army suit.

"I guess she's going to be pretty late again tonight, Jim," the old man said in a squeaky voice. "Do you think it's the snow?"

"I don't know," the other man said, sounding somewhat annoyed. The steam of his breath disappeared beneath his thick, wild red beard.

"It's not likely that anybody from the East will be coming with the corpse, I suppose," the old man said.

"I don't know," the bearded man said again.

"It's too bad he didn't belong to some lodge or other," the old man went on. "I like an order funeral myself. They seem more fitting for well-known people."

Just then a train whistle sounded in the distance. There was a sudden shuffling of feet on the platform. Then a number of tall boys appeared. Some of them came from the waiting room, where they'd been warming themselves by the stove. Two more climbed down from the driver's seat of a hearse that was next to the platform.

In a moment the train's bright headlight streamed up the snow-covered track. The big man with the red beard walked quickly up the platform toward the oncoming train. The group of men behind him looked at one another, and then followed his example. The train stopped. The crowd shuffled up to one of the cars just as the door was thrown open. The train conductor appeared in the doorway. Standing next to him was a young man in a long overcoat and a cap.

"Are Mr. Merrick's friends here?" the young man asked.

The group on the platform swayed and shuffled. Philip Phelps, the banker, answered for them. "We have come to take charge of the body. Mr. Merrick's father is ill and can't get around much."

The coffin was taken down from the train and placed on the snowy platform. No one said a thing. The young man who had come with the body looked about him. He was a stranger from Boston, and he had been one of the dead sculptor's pupils. He turned to the banker, the only one of the group who seemed likely to give him an answer.

"None of Mr. Merrick's brothers are here?" he asked.

The heavy man with the red beard stepped up for the first time and joined the group. "No, they have not come yet," he said. "The family is spread out in different parts of the country. The body will be taken right to the house." And with that he bent down and took hold of one of the coffin's handles.

The coffin was loaded onto the hearse. Then the undertaker snapped the door shut and climbed up in the driver's seat.

Laird, the red-bearded lawyer, turned once again to the young stranger. "It's a long walk, so you'd better go up in the hack." He pointed to a run-down carriage.

"Thank you, but I think I will go up with the hearse," the young man said. Then he turned to the undertaker. "If you don't object, I'll ride with you."

A short while later, the hearse backed up to a wooden sidewalk before a weather-beaten frame house. The men who had been at the station were now waiting at the front gate. The gate hung on one hinge and was difficult to open wide. Steavens, the young stranger, noticed that something black was tied to the knob of the front door.

As the coffin was drawn from the hearse, a scream rang out from inside the house. Then the door was thrown open and a tall, heavy woman rushed out into the snow. She threw herself on the coffin. "My boy, my boy! This is how you've come home to me!" she screamed.

Steavens turned away and closed his eyes. Then a younger woman, also tall but thin, rushed out of the house. Catching Mrs. Merrick by the shoulders, she cried out sharply, "Come, come, mother, you mustn't go on like this!" Then she calmly turned to the banker. "The living room is ready, Mr. Phelps."

The coffin was carried inside. The room was large and cold and it smelled of dampness and furniture polish. Henry Steavens stared about him with the awful feeling that some horrible mistake had been made. He wondered if he had arrived at the wrong place. Quickly he looked around for something that might have once belonged to Harvey Merrick. Finally he recognized his friend in a crayon picture of a curly-haired boy. It was hanging above the piano. Only then was Steavens willing to let any of these people come near the coffin.

"Take the lid off, Mr. Thompson," the old woman cried to the undertaker. "Let me see my boy's face."

The daughter sat stiffly upon the sofa, her hands folded in her lap. Her mouth and eyes were drawn down as she silently awaited the opening of the coffin. An older woman stood near the door. She was clearly the servant in the house. Her sad and gentle face made her look timid. She was crying silently and wiping her tears with the corner of her apron. Steavens walked over and stood beside her.

Light steps were heard on the stairs. Then an old man, tall and weak-looking, entered the room. He had shaggy, uncombed gray hair and a beard. The old man went slowly up to the coffin. He stood there quietly rolling a blue handkerchief between his hands. He seemed so upset and embarrassed by his wife's grief that he wasn't aware of anything else.

"There, there, Annie, dear, don't take on so," he said softly. She turned with a cry and sank down on his shoulder with such force that he nearly fell. As he looked at her, his cheeks slowly became red as if burning with shame. Then his wife rushed from the room, and her daughter went after her. After a moment, the servant went up to the coffin and bent over it. Then she slipped away to the kitchen. That left Steavens, the lawyer, and the old father to themselves.

The old man turned to the lawyer. "Phelps and the rest are coming back to set up with Harve, aren't they?" he asked. "Thank you, Jim, thank you." He brushed the hair back gently from his son's forehead. "He was a good boy, Jim, always a good boy," he went on. "He was gentle as a child and the kindest of them all. But none of us ever under-stood him." The tears trickled slowly down his beard and dropped on the dead sculptor's coat.

"Martin, Martin!" his wife cried from the top of the stairs.

"Yes, Annie, I'm coming," he said. He turned away and then reached back. He patted the dead man's hair softly once more and stumbled from the room.

"Poor old man. I didn't think he had any tears left," the lawyer said. "Seems as if his eyes would have gone dry long ago."

Something in his voice made Steavens look up. While the mother had been in the room, he had hardly noticed anyone else. Now he looked closely into Jim Laird's face. The face belonged to a man who was having a hard time controlling himself. He kept plucking at his beard in anger. Steavens knew that he had found what he had been heartsick at not finding before. It was the feeling, the understanding, that must exist at such a time—even here.

Suddenly loud voices could be heard from the kitchen. The mother was yelling at the servant woman. It seemed she had forgotten to make the dressing for the chicken salad which had been prepared for the watchers. Steavens had never heard anything like it. The mother's tone was dramatic and cruel. Now she was as violent in anger as she had been earlier in her grief.

"Poor Roxy's getting it now," the lawyer said. "The Merricks took her out of the poor house years ago. If she wasn't so loyal to them, she could tell tales that would curdle your blood. The old woman is half-crazed. She made Harvey's life a hell for him when he lived at home. He was so ashamed of it. I never could see how he kept himself so sweet."

"He was wonderful," Steavens said slowly. "But until tonight I never knew how wonderful."

"That is the wonder of it," the lawyer said, "that something good can come even from such a dump as this." Then he made a sweeping gesture with his arm that seemed to take in more than just the four walls.

"Did he keep much to himself back in Boston?" Laird suddenly asked. "He was very shy as a boy."

"Yes, he did," Steavens answered. "He could be very fond of people. But he always kept his distance. He disliked strong emotions. I know he thought a lot about things. And he wasn't sure of himself in many ways—except about his work. He was sure-footed enough there. He didn't trust men very much, and women even less. But he didn't believe the worst about them, either. In fact, he wanted to believe the best. But he was afraid to get close to anyone."

"A burned dog fears the fire," the lawyer said, and closed his eyes.

At 11:00 the Merricks' daughter entered the room to say that the watchers were arriving. She asked Steavens and the lawyer to "step into the dining room."

As Steavens got up, the lawyer said, "You go on. It will be a good experience for you. As for me, I'm not up to that crowd tonight. I've had 20 years of them."

The same group that had been at the train station came into the dining room. In the light of the room they stood apart and became separate people again. There was the minister, a pale, weak-looking man with white hair and blond chin-whiskers. He took a seat next to a small side table and placed a Bible on it. The old man in the Grand Army uniform sat down behind the stove. The two bankers, Phelps and Elder, walked off to a corner behind the dinner table. The coal and lumber dealer and the cattle shipper sat on opposite sides of the coal-burner.

Soon it was clear that all the family members had gone to bed. The Grand Army man was the first to speak up.

"Do you guess there will be a will, Phelps?" he asked.

"There will hardly be a need for one, will there?" The banker laughed.

"Why, the old man says Harve has done real well lately," the first man said.

The other banker spoke up. "I guess he means that Harve hasn't asked for money lately. He hasn't needed to take any more mortgages on the farm so Harve could go on with his education."

"I can't seem to remember a time when Harve wasn't being educated," the Grand Army man said.

There was general laughter. "It's too bad the old man's sons didn't turn out better," Phelps said. "They never hung together. He spent enough money on Harve to stock a dozen cattle farms. He might as well have poured it into Sand Creek. Harve should have stayed at home and helped take care of what little they had. Then they might all have been well fixed. Instead, the old man was cheated by tenants right and left."

Phelps went on. "The old man made his mistake by sending the boy East to school. That's where he got his head full of nonsense. Going off to Paris was plain foolish. What Harve needed was a course at some top business college in Kansas City."

Steavens could not believe his ears. Was it possible that these men did not understand? Who would ever have heard of their town if it hadn't been Harvey Merrick's birthplace? Steavens remembered what his master had said to him on the day of his death. It had become clear that his lungs were failing and he would not recover. It was then that the sculptor had asked his pupil to take his body home.

"It's not a nice place to be lying while the world is doing better," he'd said with a weak smile. "But in the end, it seems as though we should go back to the place we came from. The townspeople will come in for a look at me. And after they have their say, I won't have much to fear from God's judgment."

"Forty is young for a Merrick to die," the cattle man said. "They usually hang on pretty well. He probably helped it along with too much whisky."

"His mother's people don't live long," the minister said. "And Harvey never had a strong body." The minister would have liked to say more. He had been the boy's Sunday school teacher, and he had liked him. But he felt he was not in a position to speak. His own sons had turned out badly. A year ago one of them had made his last trip home on that same train. He'd been shot in a gambling house in the Black Hills.

Just then the living room door opened. Everyone was relieved when only Jim Laird came out. But his red face was filled with anger. The Grand Army man ducked his head when he saw the look on Jim's face.

"I've been with you gentlemen before," the lawyer began in a dry tone. "We have all sat by the coffins of boys born and raised in this town. And if I remember correctly, you are never too satisfied when you check them up. What's the matter anyway?

"Why is it that good young men are as hard to find as millionaires in Sand City? Look what happens to them. There was Ruben Sayer—the brightest young lawyer you ever turned out. He came home from school as straight as an arrow. Why did he take to drinking and forge a check and shoot himself? Or how about Bill Merrit's son, dying in a saloon in Omaha. And why did young Adams burn his mill to cheat the insurance companies and wind up in prison?"

The lawyer paused and placed one closed fist on the table. "I'll tell you why. Because you drummed nothing but money and greed into their ears from the time they were little boys. You held our friends Phelps and Elder up to them for their models. But the boys were young—too young for the business you put them up to. You wanted them to be successful rascals. But they weren't good at that.

"There was only one boy ever raised here who didn't turn out badly. And you hated Harvey Merrick more for winning out than you hated all the other boys who failed. God, how you hated him! Phelps likes to say he could buy and sell us all out anytime he wants to. But he knew Harve wouldn't have given him a red cent for his bank and all his cattle farms put together. And Phelps can't stand the thought of it."

The lawyer stopped for a minute and then went on. "Harvey and I went to school together back East. We were honest and serious. We wanted all of you to be proud of us some day. We meant to be great men. I came back here to be a lawyer. But then I found out you didn't want me to be a great man. You wanted me to be smart—or should I say crooked.

All of you needed a lawyer for some shady deal or another. And you'll go on needing me. That's why I'm not afraid to tell you the truth this once.

"Well, I did what you wanted. I came back here and became the crooked lawyer you wanted me to be. Now you pretend to have some kind of respect for me. Yet you'll stand up and throw mud at Harvey Merrick. You knew he was a man whose soul you couldn't dirty and whose hands you couldn't tie! Sometimes I used to like to think about him. How glad I felt that he was off there in the world, away from this dirty town. I knew he was doing his great work and climbing the big mountain he'd set for himself.

"And *we*? What have we done but fought and lied and sweated and stolen and hated? We've acted as only the disappointed strugglers in a bitter, dead little Western town know how to act. And what do we have to show for it? Harvey Merrick would not have given one sunset over your marshes for all that you have put together. You know that is true.

"I want this Boston man to know that he's been hearing a lot of garbage here tonight. But I also want him to know that it's the only tribute that could be expected. A truly great man could get nothing else from the sick, thieving men who run this town. And may God have mercy on it!"

The lawyer put his hand out to Steavens as he passed him. Then he grabbed his overcoat and left the house as quickly as he could.

The next day Jim Laird was not able to attend the funeral. Steavens called at his office and left his address. But he couldn't manage to see the lawyer before he went back East. Steavens thought he might hear from Laird in the future. But he never did.

The thing in Laird that Harvey Merrick had loved must have been buried with Merrick. Somehow it never spoke out again. Jim Laird died that same winter. He had caught a cold while driving across the Colorado mountains.

He was heading there to defend one of Phelps's sons who had gotten into trouble for selling government timber.

The Way of the World

Not many young boys have a town named after them. But Speckle knows what he's doing. At least he thought he did before Mary Eliza barged in.

THE BOY WAS A PRINCE IN HIS OWN RIGHT AND A RULER
OF MEN.

The Way of the World

O! the world was full of the summer
*   time*
And the year was always June,
When we two played together
In the days that were done too soon.

O! every hand was an honest hand,
And every heart was true.
When you were the king of the
*   cornlands*
And I was queen with you.

*When I could believe in the fairies
     still,
And our elf in the cottonwood tree,
And the pot of gold at the rainbow's
     end
And you could believe in me.*

Speckle Burnham sat on Mary Eliza's front porch, waiting for her to finish practicing. He was in no special hurry for her to do so. But his bare feet shuffled over the splintery boards when the piano playing inside became faster. That meant that Mary Eliza's "hour" was nearly over and she was rushing to get through.

Indeed, Speckle had a lot of things on his mind. The boy was a prince in his own right and a ruler of men.

In Speckle's backyard were half a dozen large store boxes. They were placed evenly in a row against the side of the barn. That was Speckle's empire. And it was a dream come true for the boys on Speckle's street. For a long time they had wanted to collect their lemonade stands and sidewalk booths to form a community. But without Speckle's leadership, it would never have been possible.

In the first place, Speckle had just about the worst backyard in the neighborhood. No other parents would have allowed the boys to litter up their yard with the boxes. But Speckle's folks had been farming people. They felt that a backyard was just the right spot for all the things that did not belong inside the house. And that included Speckle. So he had offered his yard as a place for the new town. The other boys brought their store boxes and called the town Speckleville in his honor.

Speckle kept things well organized. No boy was allowed to change his business or his location without permission from the council of Speckleville. Jimmy Templeton kept a grocery store. He carried soda crackers, ginger snaps, and "Texas Mixed." The last item was a cheap candy that came in big wooden buckets sneaked out of his own father's store.

Tommy Sanders ran a hardware store. He carried bows and arrows, slingshots, pea shooters, and ammunition for all of them. Dick Hutchinson ran the dime museum. He bravely handled live bull snakes for a small price. He also had on display snapping turtles, pocket gophers, and rusty firearms. Reinholt Birkner was the son of the village undertaker and a rather sorrowful boy. He kept a marble shop where he made little tombstones and caskets for the boys' dead pets.

Because of his many talents, Speckle held all the important offices in the town. He was the mayor and postmaster. He ran a bank where he made the boys deposit their earnings—in this case, the pins the boys used to stand for real money. He charged them a lot—both to make their deposits and when they needed to borrow funds. Speckle often threatened to take away the store of any boy who was behind in his payments. But he never followed through on his threats.

Speckle surely had the right to be a strong ruler. After all, it was his imagination, even more than his backyard, that had made that town come to be. He saw those store boxes as temples of trade. And he could make other people see what he saw. He could invent jobs for half a dozen boys. He could make up holidays and circuses and other public festivals.

It was as if he had everyone in a spell. He was like a clever stage actor who can make an audience gasp when he draws his fake sword. And like some play actors, Speckle began to believe his own role. It didn't bother him a bit that he still had to take milk door-to-door to the neighbors at night. So what if he had been scolded because he'd lost the hatchet? What did it matter that he sometimes forgot to do a chore for his father? He was the founder of a city and a king of men!

The boys of Speckleville lived together in peace and harmony—for a while. Then one day Mary Eliza Jenkins looked at them from her back porch. Peeking through the morning glory vines, she saw how happy they seemed to be, and she got mad. Even though Mary Eliza was the tomboy of the street, she was still a girl. And to her, six males living together in peace and happiness was not a natural thing. Besides, she and Speckle had played together ever since they were very little. In fact, he was closer to her than to any boy on the street. But that was before Speckleville. Since then, she had felt very angry at being deserted.

Once, on the spur of the moment, the boys had invited her over to a circus in Speckle's barn. After that, Speckle knew no peace in his life. Day and night, she begged him to let her join his town. She hung around his back porch as soon as she finished practicing her piano. She whispered to him in Sunday school. She ran up to him while he was taking his cow out to pasture. She sprang out at him when he was delivering his milk in the evening. She was everywhere.

Now, Speckle himself was not against letting Mary Eliza join the town. But the other boys would not hear of it.

"She'll try to boss all of us just like she bosses you," Tommy Sanders said.

"Anyhow, she's a girl and this town isn't for girls," Dick Hutchinson said. "I suppose she'd keep a dressmaking shop and dress our dolls for us," he snorted.

"Put it any way you like, she'll spoil the town," Jimmy Templeton said.

"You're the one who started it, Temp," Speckle had said. "*You* asked her to come to the circus—you know you did."

Now Speckle thought about all of this as he sat on Mary Eliza's porch. He had come over this morning to talk her out of trying to join the town. Now he heard a loud "one, two, three, FOUR," and then a last bang on the piano keys. A moment later Mary Eliza dashed out on the porch.

"Well, have you made them let me in?" she demanded.

Speckle braced himself and came directly to the point.

"I can't make them, Mary 'Liza. And they say you'd get tired and spoil the town."

"Oh, stuff! Why do they say that?"

"Well, it's because you're a girl, I guess," Speckle said. He wrinkled the big yellow freckle on his nose that was the reason for his nickname.

"Girl nothin'! I'd pretend I was a man, and that's all you do! *M.E. Jenkins*— that's what I'll have over my store. I've got the signs already made. *Delmonico Restaurant, M.E. Jenkins, Owner.* Come on, Speckle. You know I can skin a cat as well as you can. I can beat Hutch running, can't I?"

"Of course you can. I'd like to have you in, Mary 'Liza," Speckle answered.

"Oh, well, I don't care so much about getting in your old town anyhow. But my father runs the bakery, you know. I could have cookies and cream puffs and candy to sell in my store—none of your old Texas Mixed. I could be a good deal of use in your town."

"Say, Mary 'Liza, do you mean that? I guess I'd better tell them. I'll tell them tonight," Speckle said with new interest.

"Oh, do, Speckle, and do get me in!" cried Mary Eliza happily. "You know you can if you want to. It's *your* yard!"

Speckle did not answer at once. He was wondering whether Mary Eliza had what it takes. Could she meet the large demands on the imagination required of the residents of Speckleville? He did not know much about the female imagination. And since he didn't know how to talk about his doubts, he kept silent.

"What are you thinking about now?" Mary Eliza demanded.

"Nothing. I'll see them about it tonight," Speckle answered.

"If they don't let me in, I'll know it's all your fault," she said in a threatening way. Then she dashed into the house.

That night Speckle went around to each of the boys privately. He hoped that by seeing them alone he could best appeal to their separate weaknesses.

First he bribed Dick Hutchinson. All it took was a dozen of the tin tobacco tags his uncle had sent from Florida. He won Reinholt Birkner with promises of many fancy funerals for any of Mary Eliza's dead pets. He charmed Shorty Thompson with stories of the cream puffs from old Jenkins' bakery. Over Jimmy Templeton he had no hold. Jimmy was without any secret weaknesses. So Speckle just told him the other boys had agreed. Then he used his own powers of persuasion to get Jimmy to go along.

"All right, if you fellows say so," Temp answered. "I won't be the man to kick. But you mark my word, Speckle, she'll spoil the town. Girls always spoil everything a boy's got if you give them a chance."

That night after Speckle had climbed into bed, he heard a loud knock at the window.

"Hello, Temp, is that you?" he called.

"No, Speckle, it's me," Mary Eliza whispered. "Did you make them?"

"Yes, I made them," Speckle answered.

"Oh, Speckle, you are a dandy! I just love you, Speckle!" Mary Eliza pounded happily at the screen before she ran off.

The next day Speckle emptied his piano box, the largest and best structure in his town. Then, while his amazed friends looked on, he fitted it up perfectly for Mary Eliza. In the afternoon Mary Eliza made her grand entry into Speckleville. The boys did not greet her warmly, but she was all smiles. She showed no sign of anger at her unfriendly welcome. Then she set forth her cream puffs and chocolates and other goods. Within half an hour, the Delmonico Restaurant was the center of interest and activity.

There seemed to be no end to the things Mary Eliza did to take Speckle's place as town leader. She made it her business to appeal to every male instinct in the boys—beginning with their stomachs. The cream puffs alone would have brought her victory. But she did not stop there. Next she made wonderful neckties of colored tissue paper, and stiff hats of pasteboard covered with black paper. It wasn't long before she was the unchallenged ruler of the town.

Indeed, Mary Eliza had many talents. All of them suited her quite well to live and rule in a boys' town. Otherwise she could never have brought such disaster upon the town of Speckleville. For all boys will admit the truth: *There are some girls who would make the best boys in the world—if they were not girls.*

It wasn't long before Mary Eliza's word was law in Speckleville. Half the letters that went through Speckle's post office were for her. Even strange Reinholt Birkner fell under her spell. He made her a beautiful little tombstone with a rose carved on it for her center table.

Meanwhile, Speckle—poor Speckle— sat by sadly and watched Mary Eliza's success. And all the while he sadly remembered that he was the one who had brought her into the town.

Then, alas, tragedy came to the town of Speckleville. The heavy villain of the story came in the form of a boy from

Chicago. He had come to spend the summer with his aunt just across the street from Speckle's house.

From the beginning, the Speckleville boys didn't like him. For one thing, he wore shoes and socks. That seemed like a silly thing to do in the minds of Speckleville's citizens. To this, he added the mistake of wearing a stiff hat. And then on Sundays he made it even worse by wearing kid gloves. The good citizens of Speckleville all looked with horror upon these things—all except one person, that is.

The first time the New Boy visited the town, he bought a cream puff from Mary Eliza. When he was told that the price was ten pins, he laughed loudly. He said that he didn't carry a pincushion on him. He then threw down a nickel on the counter.

Now to offer money to a citizen of Speckleville was an insult. So the boys were painfully surprised when Mary Eliza took the shameful coin and gave him a big smile to boot.

After that, the New Boy came often. Usually he spent his money only at the Delmonico Restaurant. Then he hung about the place, bragging. He would talk about his trips to Lake Michigan and Lincoln Park while Mary Eliza listened with greedy ears. He continued to pay for his things with coins, and Mary Eliza continued to accept them with a smile. The Speckleville boys went about with a secret shame in their hearts. They felt that she had disgraced herself and them as well.

As for Mary Eliza, she by no means shared the boys' dislike for the New Boy. She thought that his city clothes and good manners were something to be admired. She even felt more grown up and important when she was in his company.

Things went from bad to worse in the town. The days came and went as days will. But the shadow of the New Boy was always hanging over Mary Eliza's throne. Finally the problem came to a head at a meeting of the town council. Mary Eliza boldly suggested admitting the New Boy to the town. Her suggestion was greeted by angry howls and hisses, and Speckle blushed to the roots of his red hair.

"Very well," Mary Eliza said. "If you won't have him in, then *I* won't be in either. The two of us will start another town over in his yard."

"You can just go and do it, then!" howled councilman Sanders. "We won't have that city boy hanging around here any longer!"

To this last comment, all the boys shouted in loud agreement.

Mary Eliza rose with great dignity and began to pack her things. She did not seem angry. She spoke cheerfully of her new town as she wrapped up her candies in tissue paper. The boys stood by silently and watched her. They did not believe she would go. But Mary Eliza left as she had come, this time with a grand exit. Speckle even held the gate open for her.

"I'll send over for my store box in the morning, Speckle," she said. "You must all come over to our town and buy things. And we'll come over and buy things at yours," she called after him.

"She'll be back tomorrow, all right," Speckle said.

But the next day the New Boy came for the piano box. By noon Mary Eliza was set up across the street. She was busy making neckties for the New Boy. Getting business for the New Boy's town was taking all her time. It was clear now that her loyalty had changed.

The Speckleville boys went back to their stores. They bought and sold and made a great show. But they had no heart in it. They missed the cream puffs and the paper ties. And they missed something else even more—something they could not name.

Mary Eliza had put herself at the head of everything. And now nothing went on without her. She had come where she was not wanted, made herself needed by everyone, and then she had gone again.

But what she took away with her was so much more than cream puffs and chocolate creams!

Everything went wrong in Speckleville that afternoon. After the day was over, the citizens of that village were having major arguments with each other.

"It's all your fault, Speckle! We should never have let her in. And we wouldn't— if it hadn't been for you."

"Well, now she's gone," Speckle said. "Why can't we just go on like we did before?"

No one tried to answer. It wasn't a wise question to ask.

"I always told you she'd spoil the town, Speckle. And now she's done it!" Jimmy Templeton said.

"Well, you fellows seemed mighty glad she was here," Speckle answered. "And *you* don't have to say a word, Temp," he added. "You hung around her store like a ninny all the time."

Jimmy was in no mood to put up with a stab at his weakness. So instead of an answer, he punched Speckle on the side of his nose. It took the combined strength of all the other boys to pull them apart.

"I'm not going to stay in your old town any longer," Dick Hutchinson announced. "I can have more fun in my own yard. I'm going to take my things home."

"Me, too," cried Jimmy Templeton. "And I'll thank you to give me my pins out of your tin box, Mr. Speckle."

Speckle had enough trouble without a run on his bank. But he had no choice. He sat there until he had paid out the last pin from his box. The boys all started to pack their things as if they were fleeing from a doomed city. Under Speckle's very eyes, his town vanished as many another western town has done.

That night Speckle could hear Mary Eliza laughing. He saw that she was playing tag under the street light with the New Boy. Speckle sat down with his empty milk pails in his deserted town. Like many an overturned ruler before him, he was a lonely king without a kingdom.

Thinking About
the Stories

Paul's Case

1. Who is the main character in this story? Who are one or two of the minor characters? Describe each of these characters in one or two sentences.

2. Good writing always has an effect on the reader. How did you feel when you finished reading this story? Were you surprised, horrified, amused, sad, touched, or inspired? What elements in the story made you feel that way?

3. Suppose this story had a completely different outcome. Can you think of another effective ending for this story?

The Sculptor's Funeral

1. Are there friends or enemies in this story? Who are they? What forces do you think keep the friends together and the enemies apart?

2. Some stories are packed with action. In other stories, the key events take place in the minds of the characters. Is this

story told more through the characters' thoughts and feelings? Or is it told more through their outward actions?

3. All stories fit into one or more categories. Is this story serious or funny? Would you call it an adventure, a love story, or a mystery? Is it a character study? Or is it simply a picture the author has painted of a certain time and place? Explain your thinking.

The Way of the World

1. Compare and contrast at least two characters in this story. In what ways are they alike? In what ways are they different?

2. All the events in a story are arranged in a certain order, or sequence. Tell about one event from the beginning of this story, one from the middle, and one from the end. How are these events related?

3. The plot is the series of events that takes place in a story. Usually, story events are linked in some way. Can you name an event in this story that was the cause of a later event?